Christmas

Around the World

Christmas in France

by Kristin Thoennes

Consultant:
Françoise Gramet

Hilltop Books

an imprint of Franklin Watts
A Division of Grolier Publishing
New York London Hong Kong Sydney
Danbury, Connecticut

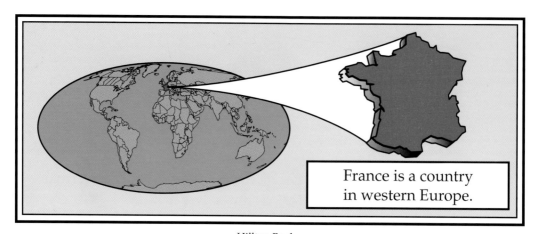

France is a country
in western Europe.

Hilltop Books
http://publishing.grolier.com
Copyright © 1999 by Capstone Press • All rights reserved
Published simultaneously in Canada• Printed in the United States of America

Library of Congress Cataloging-in-Publication Data
Thoennes, Kristin.
    Christmas in France/by Kristin Thoennes.
    p. cm.—(Christmas around the world)
    Includes bibliographical references (p. 24) and index.
    Summary: An overview of the symbols, celebrations, decorations, food, and songs that are part of
Christmas in France.
    ISBN 0-7368-0088-3
    1. Christmas—France—Juvenile literature. 2. France—Social life and customs—Juvenile literature.
[1. Christmas—France. 2. France—Social life and customs. 3. Holidays.] I. Title. II. Series.
GT4987.48.T48 1999
394.2663'0944—dc21
                                                                                    98-15743
                                                                                        CIP
                                                                                         AC

Editorial Credits
Cara Van Voorst, editor; James Franklin, cover designer and illustrator; Sheri Gosewisch, photo researcher

Photo Credits
Ange/Wallis, 12
P. Somelet/DIAF, 14
Photo Researchers/A. Autenzio, 16
Photri, 10, 18
Trip Photo Library/Ask Images, 4, 20; B. Gadsby, cover
Unicorn Stock Photos/Martha McBride, 6; Joel Dexter, 8

Table of Contents

Christmas in France

Many people around the world celebrate Christmas. Celebrate means to do something enjoyable on a special occasion. People in different countries celebrate Christmas in different ways.

France is a country in western Europe. French people live in France. They speak the French language. Their Christmas greeting is Joyeux Noël (jwah-YEUH no-EL). It means "Happy Christmas."

People celebrate Christmas Day on December 25. But Christmas in France starts on December 6. December 6 is the feast of Saint Nicholas. Christmas celebrations in France end with Epiphany. Epiphany is on January 6.

The weather during Christmas is different all over France. It is cold and snowy in the north. It is mild and sunny in the south. Mild means days are warm and nights are cool.

Christmas in France begins on December 6.

The First Christmas

Christmas is a celebration of Jesus Christ's birthday. Many people who celebrate Christmas are Christians. Christians follow the teachings of Jesus Christ.

Jesus' parents were Mary and Joseph. They traveled to a city called Bethlehem. They wanted to find a room at an inn. An inn is like a hotel. All the rooms in Bethlehem's inns were full. Mary and Joseph had to find another place to stay.

Mary and Joseph stayed in a stable. A stable is a place where people keep animals. Jesus was born in the stable. Mary and Joseph filled a manger with straw. A manger is a box that holds food for animals. Jesus slept in the manger.

Three kings saw a star the night Jesus was born. They followed the star to the stable in Bethlehem. The kings honored Jesus with gifts and praise.

Jesus slept in a manger.

Crèches

The crèche (KRESH) is a symbol of Christmas in France. A symbol is an object that reminds people of something important. A crèche is a nativity scene. A nativity scene shows the birth of Jesus. The crèche reminds French people of Jesus' birth.

Many crèches include figurines. A figurine is a small, molded figure. The French call these figures santons (sahn-TOHN). Santons are made from terra-cotta (TER-uh KOT-uh). Terra-cotta is a hard, waterproof clay. People paint the figures by hand. Most santons look like people or animals. Some santons are of Mary, Joseph, and Jesus. Others are of shepherds or kings.

People set up crèches in many places during Christmas in France. Church members often set up crèches in their churches weeks before Christmas. Sometimes live actors appear in large crèches. Most families have small crèches at home.

Sometimes live actors appear in large crèches.

Decorations

Flowers are a common Christmas decoration in France. Many people put flowers on tables. Visitors often bring flowers. The French people especially like roses, carnations, and snapdragons as decorations.

The sapin de Noël (sah-PEH DUH no-EL) is another Christmas decoration. Sapin is the French word for fir tree. More French people decorate with Christmas trees than in the past. They sometimes use potted trees. French people plant the trees outside after the Christmas season.

French people decorate their Christmas trees with ornaments and lights. An ornament is a decoration people hang on Christmas trees. Ornaments may be bulbs, bells, or angels.

People can buy santons in many places in France at Christmas time. They make different Christmas scenes with the santons.

People can buy santons in many places in France at Christmas time.

Christmas Celebrations

French people celebrate many days during the Christmas season. The first day they celebrate is the feast of Saint Nicholas. It is on December 6. Saint Nicholas was the saint of children. He helped poor children. Children often receive candy or other treats on Saint Nicholas Day.

Most French people celebrate on Christmas Eve. They go to midnight church services. A meal called réveillon (reh-vay-OHN) follows the services. Réveillon means to wake up.

Many French people also celebrate the day of Epiphany. It is on January 6. Some people call this day the Three Kings Day. This is the day the three kings first saw Jesus. Many French people give gifts and attend church on Epiphany. They also eat a special treat called the Cake of Kings.

Children often receive candy or other treats on Saint Nicholas Day.

Père Noël

Most French children believe in Père Noël (PEHR no-EL). Père Noël means Father Christmas. Père Noël is a tall, thin man. He has a white beard and wears a long, red robe. Père Noël carries a sack of treats and toys for children. A donkey sometimes helps Père Noël carry his sack.

Many French children leave snacks for Père Noël on Christmas Eve. They also leave food for his donkey.

French children write letters to Père Noël at the North Pole. Children use polite language in the letters. They ask Père Noël for gifts.

Many French children believe that Père Noël has a helper. The helper is Père Fouettard (PEHR foo-TARD). This means Father Whipper. Père Fouettard tells Père Noël which children do not behave.

Père Noël carries a sack of treats and toys for children.

Christmas Presents

Some people in France believe Père Noël comes twice. He brings small gifts and candy treats for children on December 6. That day is the feast of Saint Nicholas.

Père Noël also comes on Christmas Eve. Some children put their shoes near the fireplace on Christmas Eve. Others put their shoes near the crèche or the Christmas tree. They hope Père Noël will fill them with presents.

Most children receive toys, games, and candy as presents. The children open their gifts on Christmas Day.

Adults open their gifts on New Year's Day. New Year's Day is January 1. Many people also give presents to helpers in the community. Helpers may be butchers or letter carriers.

Some children put their shoes near the fireplace on Christmas Eve. They hope Père Noël will fill them with gifts.

Holiday Foods

The French do not have traditional foods for their Christmas meals. Traditional means a practice continued over many years. French people eat many kinds of foods during Christmas. Some French people eat roasted goose. Others eat turkey and chestnuts. Oysters are the favorite Christmas food in Paris.

Réveillon is the Christmas Eve supper. Réveillon lasts many hours. Families may eat small helpings of many foods.

French people burned a large log for Christmas in the past. They called it a yule log. Yule is another word for Christmas. Most people today no longer burn a yule log.

Today, many French people eat a cake shaped like a yule log. The French call the cake bûche de Noël (BOOSH DUH no-EL). It is a sponge cake with chocolate filling. Bakers make the cake's frosting look like real bark.

Today, many French people eat a cake shaped like a yule log.

Noëls and Pastorales

Noëls are French Christmas songs. One famous Christmas song from France is "Oh, Holy Night." Placide Clappeau wrote the words to the song in 1847. He was a sales person and a mayor.

French people also sing other popular Christmas songs. They sing "Les Enfants Oubliés" and "Glory Glory Alleluia." They also sing "Noël Nouvelet." It means "Christmas Comes Anew."

Many people in France celebrate Christmas with pastorales. A pastorale is a musical show. People act, sing, and dance in pastorales. The pastorales take place in theaters, concert halls, and churches.

The French also put on Christmas plays. They dress like people from the Christmas story. Live animals also may be in these plays.

Many people in France celebrate Christmas with pastorales.

Hands on: Make a Christmas Cracker

French children make Christmas crackers. The crackers are papers filled with candy. Children call them crackers because the papers make noise when they are opened. You can make a Christmas cracker.

What You Need

gold or silver gift-wrap paper

scotch tape

scissors

a ruler

small candies

a pencil

brightly colored ribbon

What You Do

1) Cut a piece of paper 10 inches (25 centimeters) long by six inches (15 centimeters) wide.
2) Overlap the two long sides about one-half inch (one centimeter). Tape these ends together. This forms a tube.
3) Slide a small amount of candy into the center of the tube.
4) Twist each end of the paper. The twist should be about three inches (eight centimeters) from each end.
5) Tie each twist with a ribbon.
6) Hold one end of the cracker. Offer the other end to a friend. Pull the ends until the cracker splits and spills the candies.

Words to Know

celebrate (SEL-uh-brate)—to do something enjoyable on a special occasion

Christian (KRISS-chuhn)—a person who follows the teachings of Jesus Christ

crèche (KRESH)—the French word for nativity scene

figurine (fig-yur-EEN)—a small, molded figure

Joyeux Noël (jwah-YEUH no-EL)—the French phrase for Happy Christmas

manger (MAYN-jur)—a food box for animals

ornament (OR-nuh-muhnt)—a decoration hung on a Christmas tree

pastorale (pahss-tohr-AHL)—a musical show in France

Père Noël (PEHR no-EL)—the French Father Christmas

réveillon (reh-vay-OHN)—the French Christmas Eve meal

sapin de Noël (sah-PEH DUH no-EL)—the French word for Christmas tree

stable (STAY-buhl)—a building where people keep animals

symbol (SIM-buhl)—an object that reminds people of something important

Read More

Christmas in France. Christmas around the World from World Book. Chicago: World Book, 1996.

Kennedy, Pamela. *A Christmas Celebration: Traditions and Customs from Around the World.* Nashville: Ideals Children's Books, 1992.

Lankford, Mary. *Christmas Around the World.* New York: Morrow Junior Books, 1995.

Useful Addresses and Internet Sites

The Embassy of France
4101 Reservoir Road NW
Washington, DC 20007

Maison de la France
30 St. Patrick Street
Suite 700
Toronto, ON M5T 3A3

Christmas around the World
http://www.santas.net/aroundtheworld.htm
Christmas in France
http://www.qacps.k12.md.us/ces/FRANCE.HTM
Christmas in France!
http://www.peders.com/christmas/france.html

Index